OPERATION DESERT STORM

The Invasion of Kuwait and the Second Gulf War

Written by Gilles Rahier
In collaboration with Mathieu Roger
Translated by Carly Probert

History **50MINUTES**.com

OPERATION DESERT STORM

KEY INFORMATION

- **When:** 17 January – 28 February 1991
- **Where:** In Kuwait, Iraq and Saudi Arabia
- **Context:** The Second Gulf War (1990-1991)
- **Belligerents:** Iraq against the international coalition, supported by the UN
- **Commanders and leaders:**
  - Norman Schwarzkopf, U.S. General (1932-2012)
  - Saddam Hussein, Iraqi statesman (1937-2006)
- **Outcome:** Victory for the international coalition
- **Victims:**
  - Iraqi camp: Between 80 000 and 100 000 dead and 60 000 wounded (military losses only)
  - International coalition camp: 240 dead and 776 wounded

INTRODUCTION

In August 1990, the invasion of Kuwait, which is one of the largest oil fields in the world, frightened the United Nations, the Western countries and the Middle East. The perpetrator was none other than its neighbor, Iraq, the second largest producer of world reserves of this precious liquid. This event was the catalyst of the Second Gulf War between the international coalition, supported by the UN, and Iraq, led by the dictator Saddam Hussein with an iron fist.

From 17 January to 28 February 1991, Operation Desert

Storm took place, the only battle in which the international coalition intervened during the second conflict in the Gulf. In just four days, they managed to oust the Iraqi army from Kuwait, demonstrating the superiority of the coalition forces over their Iraqi counterparts, but especially highlighting the true weakness of the latter.

Despite its short duration, this would forever remain in collective memory as the largest Allied mobilization undertaken since the Second World War (1939-1945), with the commitment of hundreds of thousands of soldiers, several thousand tanks and over a thousand aircrafts.

Defeated, Iraq finally agreed to surrender to the United Nations, causing internal uprisings in the north and the south, permanently modifying the global political situation – especially due to the importance taken by the United States – and plunging the country into an unprecedented economic and social crisis.

POLITICAL AND SOCIAL CONTEXT

THE REASONS FOR THE INVASION OF KUWAIT

Operation Desert Storm took place in the context of a conflict that was later called the Second Gulf War, fought between an international coalition of 34 countries, supported by the United Nations (UN), and led by the United States.

GOOD TO KNOW

The UN is an international organization, whose purpose is to maintain peace and global security. Founded in 1945 at the end of the Second World War, it replaced the League of Nations (LN), which was formed as a result of the First World War (1914-1918). Its general assembly brings together almost all independent countries. To facilitate cooperation between the different states, the UN has many organs, such as the Economic and Social Council, the General Secretariat, UNESCO (Educational, Scientific and Cultural Organization), UNICEF (for children) and the International Court of Justice in The Hague (Netherlands). The most important body is the Security Council, which is responsible for maintaining peace and international security. The great powers (China, USA, Russia, France and Britain) are permanently represented and have the power of veto. Added to these countries are ten non-permanent members who obtain a mandate of two years.

In 1990, Iraq was on the brink of financial abyss. Weakened by the war against Iran (1980-1988), the country was left with its oil, industrial and communication infrastructure largely destroyed. Damage was estimated at $67 billion and oil revenues were not high enough to influence the economic situation, which was becoming worse: the debt contracted by the state in order to wage war was around 80 billion dollars. Inflation was slowly growing and unemployment remained high. The boom experienced by the country during the seventies, during which it enjoyed a hegemonic position in the Middle East, was well and truly over.

For the past 11 years, Saddam Hussein was at the head of the country. Gradually, he transformed the presidential power into a true totalitarian and repressive dictatorship.

Due to the deep crisis in his country, he decided not to pay the debt of $15 billion that it owed to its neighbor, Kuwait. In support of his decision, he said during his speech that the war against the "Persian enemy" (i.e. Iran) must not be paid by Iraq alone, since through this fight it was defending the Arab world as a whole.

Meanwhile, the Emirate of Kuwait increased its oil production by 20% unilaterally without consulting OPEC, while, in order to maintain the price of crude oil, OPEC had set a production quota per country, calculated in barrels. Therefore, Kuwait made the oil prices fall on the stock market and Iraq thus lost two thirds of its annual revenues. Saddam accused the Emir Jaber al-Ahmad al-Sabah (1926-2006) of being at the source of an unprecedented social crisis.

Emir Jaber al-Ahmad al-Sabah.

There is also another older reason that may explain this invasion. Since the independence of Kuwait (1961), the Iraqi governments had been demanding the annexation of the country to their international territory. Indeed, there was an ongoing dispute over the demarcation of borders between the two countries, which were not suitable for Iraq, since it did not benefit from direct access to the Persian Gulf.

THE FIRST PHASE OF THE CONFLICT: IRAQ-KUWAIT ALTERCATION

All of these elements showed that a conflict between the two nations was imminent. Aware of the prevailing state of tension, the United States, the first world power since the collapse of the Soviet Union and the end of the Cold War (1945-1990), stated that they would not intervene in a conflict between the two Arab countries.

The trigger of the confrontation was a drilling dispute that occurred at the border in Rumaila. The Kuwait society was accused of stealing oil from an oil field located beneath the Iraqi territory by drilling diagonally. In response, on 2 August 1990, the Iraqi army entered Kuwait and took control of the country without facing any significant resistance. The territory was immediately declared the 19th Iraqi province by Saddam Hussein, who did not realize the international impact that this incursion would have, as explained by French journalist Serge July: "He lit a wick which was not intended to detonate an international crisis [...]. He never believed that a raid on this piece of oil-soaked desert would provoke such a planetary din" (July 1991). A brutal and bloody occupation of the country thus began.

THE SECOND PHASE: UN INTERVENTION AND OPERATION DESERT SHIELD

The Iraqi leader believed it was unlikely that the UN would intervene directly in the dispute and that the United States would not want to engage in another conflict overseas. However, the reaction of the UN Security Council was quick. It condemned Iraq, arguing the violation of a sovereign and independent territory of one of its members. Of the 13 resolutions passed during the Iraq crisis, three important decisions were immediately adopted during the month of August 1990:

- Resolution 660, which demanded the immediate withdrawal of Iraqi troops from Kuwait territory;
- Resolution 661, which implemented a triple embargo on Iraq on military equipment, consumer products and the export of oil;
- Finally, Resolution 665, which set up a maritime embargo and authorized the use of force.

Given this explosive situation, the United States decided to move into the Middle East from 6 August. At the request of Saudi Arabia, which feared being the next victim of Iraqi expansionism, an American contingent was sent with a large number of military devices. Operation Desert Shield began.

Under these circumstances, Iraq could not count on the help of its historic neighbors. The Arab League (religious organization grouping 21 countries), which had supported Iraq in the war against Iran, strongly condemned the invasion. At the summit of 10 August, it even decided to send a pan-Arab force to accompany the international coalition that was being formed in Saudi Arabia.

The state could not hope for the intervention of a former ally, the Soviet Union, either. In complete disarray after the fall of the Berlin Wall (1989) and faced with internal problems, it followed the course of action dictated by the West and joined forces with the United States for the first time in 45 years. It therefore did not use its veto in the Security Council, which would nevertheless have allowed it to block the sanctions and curb the international intervention in Iraq.

For Saddam Hussein, who had underestimated the impact of his actions and was now isolated on the international scene and the victim of an embargo, the situation was complicated. Moreover, he shocked the global public by promising retaliation on the western population in Kuwait, a threat at the origin of the "hostage crisis".

Meanwhile, in Saudi Arabia, the coalition was preparing and structuring its military intervention. At the request of the UN, it finally united 34 nations. This internationalization of the conflict gave the United States, the main point guard, another justification for their intervention in Kuwait.

GOOD TO KNOW

The 34 nations participating in the fighting at different levels were: Argentina, Australia, Bahrain, Bangladesh, Belgium, Canada, Denmark, Egypt, the United Arab Emirates, the United States, France, Great Britain (England, Scotland, Northern Ireland and Wales), Greece, Italy, Kuwait, Morocco, New Zealand, Niger, Norway, Oman, the Netherlands, Pakistan, Portugal, Qatar, Saudi Arabia, Senegal, Sierra Leone, Singapore, South Korea, Spain and Syria.

Finally, Resolution 678, adopted on 29 November, required the removal of Iraqi troops before 15 January 1991 and "[authorized] Member States [...] to use all necessary means to uphold and implement resolution 660 [...] and to restore international peace and security in the area". In the case of an unfavorable reply or after the deadline, the coalition would have the right to intervene.

In December and January, the latest diplomatic negotiations between the UN and Iraq did not succeed. The operation, desired by both sides, was finally launched at dawn on 17 January 1991 and was broadcast live on CNN.

GOOD TO KNOW

Missiles rained down on Tel Aviv during the nighttime bombings of Baghdad, Tomahawk cruise missiles were launched from buildings near the Iraqi coast and the scenes flooded televisions screens in 1991. Given the glut of images from both the U.S. armed forces and from CNN, the European media saw it as an opportunity to provide viewers with continuous information in real time. The idea was certainly commendable, but was not accompanied by any critical apparatus.

This wish to make the conflict more acceptable to public opinion was reflected particularly in the vocabulary used by the armed forces, which would also be used by the Western media. Therefore, people no longer spoke of "blunders", but of "collateral damage" and the term "bombing" gave way to the expression of "surgical strikes".

COMMANDERS AND LEADERS

SADDAM HUSSEIN, IRAQI STATESMAN

Saddam Hussein, 1979.

Saddam Hussein was the president of Iraq from 1979 to 2003. A leader of the Baath Party, in power from 1968, he installed a repressive and totalitarian dictatorship. Having launched the war against Iran, he decided to attack Kuwait and, thus, caused the Second Gulf War. Throughout the period before the military operations, and despite the offers of peace and negotiation, he decided not to withdraw from the conquered countries, preferring military confrontation. Experts recognized that his main mistake was choosing the warrior solution and traditional warlike tactics, while the forces present and technology did not go in his favor.

Devoid of military education (he proclaimed himself Marshal *ad honorem*) and leading the different structures of the state with an iron fist, he showed his wish to establish a long war to deter the international coalition from intervening. He turned Kuwait into an entrenched camp in an attempt to trap the opposing armies in a long struggle, knowing his only advantage lay in the significance of his land army.

During the battle, he often chose political options, his military choices being limited. He hoped to raise the Arab cause, particularly by bombing Israel and declaring *jihad* (holy war rallying the Arab peoples together against their enemies).

He remained in power after the war until 2003, when a coalition led by the United States and the United Kingdom deposed him during the third Gulf War (2003-2006). He was judged by an Iraqi Special Tribunal in July 2004 for crimes against humanity and was executed in 2006.

HERBERT NORMAN SCHWARZKOPF, U.S. GENERAL

Herbert Norman Schwarzkopf was an American general. During the invasion of Kuwait, he directed the CENTCOM (U.S. command in charge of the Middle East and Southwest Asia). He was then appointed commander of the U.S.

command center by U.S. President George H.W. Bush (born in 1924) and directed the coalition forces during Operation Desert Shield and Operation Desert Storm alongside Colin Luther Powell (born in 1937), Chief of Staff and the principal military adviser to the president.

General Herbert Norman Schwarzkopf (right) and general Colin Powell (left) during a press conference in February 1991.

Before the invasion, he prepared the defense plans of the oil fields of the Gulf against a hypothetical attack on Iraq. Under these circumstances, these plans were the basis for the future military operations of the Gulf War. Through his words, we can understand the strategy he adopted: "I will do everything to destroy the enemy brutally and as quickly as possible" (*Le Nouvel Observateur* 2012). The main objective was to not freely risk the lives of the soldiers under his command in ill-prepared operations.

His action plan was to set up a double attack: first, a constant bombardment to undermine enemy infrastructure and morale; then, when they were sufficiently weakened, a quick and precise attack with ground troops to quickly end the battle. With his meticulous preparations, the war ended in just four days.

He retired in August 1991, just months after the end of the Gulf War. He became a consultant for NBC during the Iraq war in 2003, and died in 2012.

ANALYSIS OF THE BATTLE

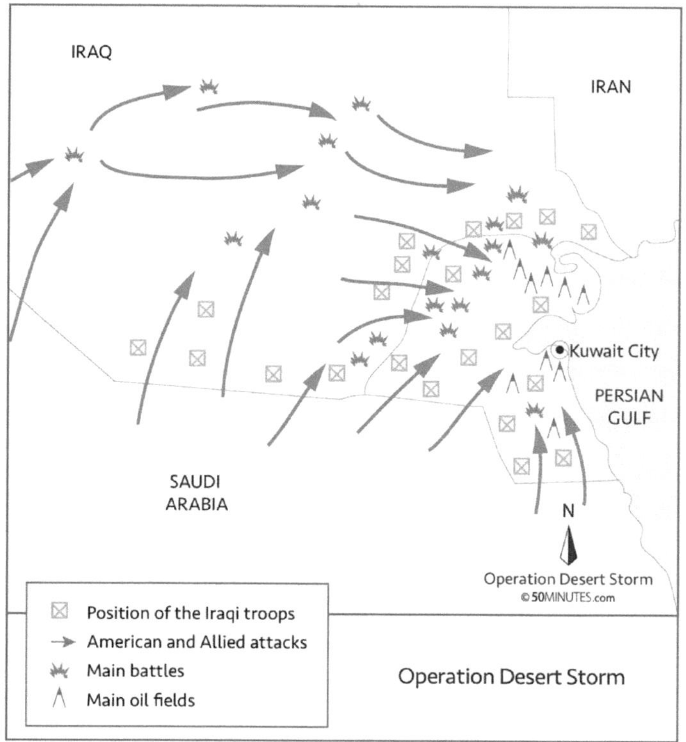

THE THIRD PHASE OF THE GULF WAR: OPERATION DESERT STORM

On 17 January 1991, the confrontation was inevitable. In the opinion of American command, the mission would be complicated because the Iraqi forces willing to fight were numerous.

In Saudi Arabia, near the border, around 700 000 men (500 000 Americans), 1 000 tanks, 1 500 helicopters and 1 300 airplanes of the international coalition gathered to liberate Kuwait. This was the largest international concentration of men, the majority of which were American, since World War II.

Pilot ready for takeoff during Operation Desert Storm, February 1991.

In the opposition camp, the Iraqis were ready to fight fiercely on the battlefield. The propaganda of their leader was clear: it would be "the mother of all battles". Their army, represented as the fourth military power in the world, had modern equipment and the experience of a previous war. According to different sources, it consisted of 500 thousand men, 5 000 armored tanks and 3 000 artillery pieces which had to defend a territory of 500 kilometers stretching from southern Iraq to Kuwait.

The battle began on 17 January 1991, and included two steps:

- 17 January to 23 February involved preparing the ground offensive through constant aerial bombardment;
- From 24-28 February the ground offensive took place (Operation Desert Storm).

THE AIR ATTACK: "CARPET BOMBING"

The coalition troops initially sent a special squadron, which carried out a raid behind enemy lines to destroy the anti-aircraft batteries. The mission opened a breach of nearly 10km in the anti-aircraft system. In this space, aviation and missiles were able to hit the heart of the Baghdad military system.

The Iraqi air force did not measure up to the advanced military presence of its opponents and was very quickly exceeded by the number of devices and the quality of their weaponry. Iraq was quickly put out of action. The first battle, which was surely the most important, was won. The occupation of the airspace was exclusively in the hands of the UN, which allowed them to bludgeon heavy damage on their opponent.

The purpose of the strikes was twofold: to directly attack Iraq's resources (military industrial complex, roads, and government buildings) and to thus weaken the entire military system and cut off the supply routes of the Iraqi ground forces defending Kuwait. In mid-February, the coalition looked to these, bombarding the defense line on the border with Saudi Arabia. Fortifications and tanks were targeted, as they were crucial elements of the Iraqi defense system. Lacking support and finding itself almost unable to fight back, the Iraqi infantry waited for 38 days, entrenched in fortifications, for the ground attack of the multinational force.

In the five weeks of fighting, nearly 90 000 tons of bombs were dropped by the international coalition. They bombarded the enemy positions relentlessly and tirelessly, with an infernal pace and intensity. The Iraqi defenses in Kuwait were barely able to resist the carpet bombing. Their only response, which involved sending missiles to the encampments in Saudi Arabia, did not cause any real damage.

On 26 January, Iraq invaded the city of Kafji, located in the territory controlled by the international coalition in Saudi Arabia. After two days of intense battles, the Iraqi divisions were chased away at the cost of many losses (approximately 50% of the contingent sent).

Seeking support, Saddam Hussein sent missiles to Israel in an attempt to involve the Hebrew country in the conflict and thus encourage the Arab countries to join his cause. But, Israel did not retaliate and remained neutral in the conflict: the operation was a failure.

Given the catastrophic situation the country was in, the Iraqi leader finally accepted the peace plan proposed by the USSR on 23 February. The United States then issued him with a 24-hour ultimatum to evacuate Kuwait. However, on

24 February, he still had not abandoned the territory and, by order of the Allied High Command, the ground offensive was triggered.

THE 100-HOUR GROUND ATTACK

The plan drawn up by General Herbert Normal Schwarzkopf was based on the encirclement of the Iraqi army, starting from along the Kuwaiti and Iraqi border and heading south to the Persian Gulf, and in the north to the central area of Iraq. The goal was to cut off the retreat of the army to Iraq.

Before the end of the ultimatum, the Allied armed forces gathered at the border with Kuwait and positioned themselves in front of the Iraqi defenses in order to make them believe that they would enter that zone directly. However, much of the coalition troops then produced a great encircling movement through the Arabian Desert to the northwest, in order to hit their left flank and cut off their retreat. Therefore, they attacked the Iraqis from behind and isolated their rear bases to prevent their reserves from reaching the front.

When the assault was given, two divisions of the Marine Corps and the contingent of the Arab forces came to Kuwait and headed for the center to release the capital (Kuwait City). Several armored and mechanized divisions received the order to break through the main defenses, and to move northwards to complete the encirclement. The plan was a success according to the Americans: of the 43 Iraqi divisions that defended the field, 26 were destroyed or re-routed in just two days.

Firmly believing that the coalition forces would be content with just liberating the occupied country, Saddam Hussein's generals had installed two parallel lines of defense of 500km in length along the border between Kuwait and Saudi Arabia. However, they had underestimated the prior work of carpet bombing, and the military defenses that had been so celebrated by the current regime and the international powers were quickly undone when faced with the tanks of the coalition. The retreat was therefore launched.

THE WITHDRAWAL OF THE IRAQI TROOPS

The rapid destruction of the Iraqi armed forces was due to several mistakes made by the High Command:

- On the front, the Iraqi ground forces remained limited to conscripts, i.e. civilians were called up for military service, while the Republican Guard (elite professional body) was almost entirely held in reserve.
- The troops on the front lines were not made up of professional soldiers, but men who were disillusioned and tired from the eight years of war against Iran. Moreover, despite appearances, they had neither the desire nor the means to fight against a better trained and better led strike force. For a month, they were in the middle of constant bombing, malnourished and often separated from their command by the destruction of communications. In fact, having barely just begun, the offensive caused the desertion of about 90 000 men.

While global public opinion expected an epic battle in the

desert, the ground attack swept up the Iraqis within hours. The coalition forces advanced quickly, repelled and pursued the Iraqi Republican Guard out of Kuwait, including through the "Highway of Death". In four days, they had occupied southern Iraq and recovered all of Kuwait. They were then able to knock on the doors of Baghdad.

Good to know

Route 80, nicknamed the "Highway of Death" was a road that connected southern Iraq to Kuwait. During the retreat of the Iraqi ground troops, on 27 February 1991, without aviation to assist them, the tanks and armored vehicles were left to the mercy of the U.S. Air Force, which included the use of depleted uranium ammunitions. An estimated 2 000 war machines were destroyed in the attack and left behind by the Iraqis. The total number of victims, whether civilian or military, would never be counted.

Military and civilian vehicles destroyed by the bombing attacks.

Photographs of the mass of destroyed vehicles have remained one of the symbolic images of the Iraqi defeat. The attack was quickly criticized in the international community – the Geneva Convention prohibited the attack on retreating troops – and, the next day, President George W. Bush was pushed to cease hostilities. The highway would be rebuilt after the war and used during the invasion of Iraq in 2003.

On 28 February 1991, the U.S. President ordered the cease-fire while Iraq announced that it accepted all of the UN resolutions unconditionally. On 3 March, the Iraqi generals signed the surrender in exchange for the withdrawal of international forces from their country. Meanwhile, the retreating army sabotaged the oil wells, thereby following the policy of scorched earth desired by the regime. The fire of 732 Kuwaiti wells also caused a major regional ecological disaster.

Kuwaiti oil wells burned by Iraqi armed forces retreat, aerial view.

Kuwaiti oil wells burned by Iraqi armed forces retreat, terrestrial view.

THE OUTCOME OF AN UNEQUAL BATTLE

From the moment the hostilities began, the Iraqi forces were in a position of inferiority. The forces were indeed disproportionate: while the international coalition used technologically advanced equipment, the Iraqis conducted classical and traditional warfare. Their forces were exceeded on air, land and naval levels, and suffered from isolation and de-motivation. This is why they did not oppose any real resistance.

During the operation, the losses on the side of the coalition were limited: there were 250 dead and 800 wounded. Many injuries were caused by friendly fire. On the Iraqi side, the

exact numbers are difficult to know, but an estimate of
85 000-100 000 deaths has been put forward.

As with the majority of wars fought by the United States,
Operation Desert Storm showed a division into stages marked by established well-defined dates and clear coordination. The goal of the American generals was to completely annihilate the armed forces of the enemy to win the battle. Unlike the Vietnam War (1954-1975), they decided to use numerous soldiers and high-performance materials to directly resist the opposing army. The deterrent effect (sustained bombardments and the large number of combatants) was the focal point of the battle.

SIGNIFICANT COLLATERAL DAMAGE

During the air operation in Iraq, bombings caused many deaths among the civilian population. The famous surgical strikes orchestrated by the U.S. military administration were not always as accurate as expected: about 70% of them missed their targets. The destruction of the water treatment plants and food processing plants caused a long-term toll on the residents, wiping out most of the infrastructure necessary for the survival of a society (water, electricity, hospitals, etc.).

Given the disastrous situation of the Iraqi population, who paid a high price for the war, international public opinion called for an end to the bombing. Some sources estimated the number of civilian deaths during the Gulf War to be 200 000.

Moreover, for the first time in history, weapons containing depleted uranium were used to destroy tanks and resilient infrastructure, such as shielding bunkers. While the intervention in Kuwait was also justified by the presence of chemical weapons held by the Iraqi regime, they were mainly used by the international coalition. The damage would affect soldiers on both sides, but also civilians. Indeed, radioactive particles from bombs were re-deposited on the soil and in the groundwater. They were inhaled by people living near the combat zones, greatly increasing the number of cases of certain diseases in the years following the battle (deformities, leukemia, etc.). This weapon also caused severe irritation of the skin and lungs and damaged the kidneys. Some experts also identified it as one of the main causes of Gulf War syndrome (immune system disorder), which affected nearly 250 000 veterans.

REPERCUSSIONS OF THE BATTLE

FOMENTING THE REVOLT

At the end of 1990, General Norman Schwarzkopf appealed to civilians to urge them to rebel and overthrow the regime. Based on a speech by President George Bush encouraging the Iraqi minorities to rise against Saddam Hussein, he would be heard at the end of the war.

From 5 March 1990, two days after the surrender, Iraq experienced an uprising of the people of Kurdistan in the north and the Shiites in the south. The protests quickly turned into an armed uprising against the Baathist regime, and later into a civil war. In one week, 15 of the 18 provinces that made up the Iraqi territory escaped from the control and the authority of Baghdad. However, despite the defeat, Saddam Hussein reacted quickly by reorganizing military units and preparing to quell the uprising.

Good to know

The Shiites are members of a religious branch of Islam, the majority of whom live in Iraq (comprising between 50-60% of the population). They are mostly found in the Middle East, Iran, Iraq, Azerbaijan and Bahrain. Supported by the Islamic Republic of Iran, led by a Shiite, Iraqi Muslims opposed the secular regime in place since the sixties, and tried several times to overthrow the Baathist administration during the dictatorship of Saddam Hussein, who harshly repressed it. After the U.S. invasion in 2003, they took a leading role in the Iraqi political reconstruction.

The Kurds are an ethnic minority, comprising some 25 million people. They are mostly represented in four Middle Eastern states: Iraq, Iran, Syria and Turkey. These nations were opposed to the creation of an independent state, Kurdistan, wanted by the Kurds since the fall of the Ottoman Empire in 1918. In Iraq, they underwent a particularly bloody repression during the dictatorship of Saddam Hussein, who repressed their separatist tendencies with chemical weapons. In 2006, the Iraqi leader was sentenced to death, accused of murdering the Kurds in Dujail (north of Baghdad). The first free elections took place in Kurdistan in 1992. The country was recognized in northern Iraq as an independent state after the fall of Saddam Hussein.

Helped by the inaction of the international coalition and the UN, who refused to intervene in an internal conflict, three divisions of the Republican Guard were in charge of the repression. They first took care of the south, then moved to the north. Lacking foreign aid, the rebel groups were disorganized, disunited and weak against the weapons of the regular Iraqi troops. The penalty was therefore exemplary and lasted four to five weeks and included atrocious brutality, the use of chemical weapons and the destruction of entire villages, causing the displacement of two million Kurdish refugees to the border of Iran and Turkey.

On 3 April, through an interpretation of Resolution 687 of the UN, the coalition countries implemented a no-fly zone over 60% of the territory, which limited the military reprisals on rebel civilians. They also set up a humanitarian operation, Operation Provide Comfort, to help these people. This did not prevent the incursions and repressions by the regime on the territories concerned.

Kurdish refugees fleeing Saddam Hussein's army thanks to allied support during Operation Provide Comfort, April 1991.

IRAQ: AN EVER-PRESENT DICTATOR AND AN UNCERTAIN FUTURE

The country found itself in an alarming situation: totally ruined by the war, it saw its economy crippled by the destruction caused by successive bombardments, the oil embargo and international sanctions. The Iraqi oil production quota was then recovered by Saudi Arabia. The embargo was therefore maintained during the Baathist regime under Resolution 687 in April 1991, and its lifting depended on the destruction of nuclear, chemical and bacteriological weapons. The inability to export oil (which represented 90% of the total exports of the country) completely destroyed the Iraqi economy, causing the gross domestic product to drop by a fifth in five years.

This country, formerly one of the richest in the region, was fast becoming impoverished, causing a humanitarian catastrophe. Indeed, the continuation of the embargo mainly affected the lower social classes.

With the establishment of the cease-fire when troops of the international coalition were close to Baghdad, the victors clearly demonstrated their desire not to topple the regime of Saddam Hussein. After the conflict, the United States and the Arab countries showed a desire to ensure the stability of the country for various reasons. The Arab countries did not accept the occupation of Iraq and preferred the solution of internal revolts. Furthermore, although the UN had authorized the use of force to expel the Iraqis from Kuwait, this was not intended to overthrow the government. The defeated regime was thus trapped in its country, completely isolated, both diplomatically and commercially.

A NEW WORLD ORDER IS ESTABLISHED

As Iraq had held a leading position along with Egypt and Saudi Arabia, by positioning itself as a protector of the secular Arab world against Islamic Iran, it was now impossible for it to fight with its neighbors, which for the most part took advantage of the oil embargo to increase their income. In the years that followed, a large flow of weapons reached the Middle East and allowed many governments to arm themselves. This arms race was already a foreshadowing of the future conflicts of the 21st century.

Furthermore, the American influence in the Middle East was affirmed by this first incursion. However, the United States decided not the settle permanently in the country, not yet undertaking their growing role as guarantors of world peace. They were seen as the "world police" at the end of the conflict. Since the upheaval that occurred in the USSR at the time of the fall of the Berlin Wall, the passivity of the latter during this event expanded the scope of the U.S., thereby choosing to expand their influence to the Middle East.

After the attacks of 11 September 2001, the United States launched a crusade against international terrorism, beginning with the Afghanistan war (began in 2001), and launched an invasion of Iraq, suspecting the possession of chemical and nuclear weapons. This is reminiscent of Resolution 687 imposed by the UN during the Second Gulf War and the U.S. refusal to overthrow the dictatorial regime of Saddam Hussein.

SUMMARY

1990
2nd Aug.: Invasion of Kuwait by Iraq
6th Aug.: Launch of Operation Desert Shield

1991
17th Jan.: Launch of Operation Desert Storm
Jan.-Feb.: Fire of 732 Kuwaiti oil wells by the Iraqis
23rd Feb.: 24-hour ultimatum issued to Iraq
24th Feb.: Ground offensive
28th Feb.: End of the operation
3rd Mar.: Signing of the surrender by Iraq

- Operation Desert Storm was the only confrontation of the Second Gulf War.
- The conflict was fought between Iraq, which invaded Kuwait, and an international coalition of 34 countries, led by the United States.
- This was the largest concentration of soldiers from various countries since World War II.
- The causes of the conflict mainly concerned the control of the oil fields in the region.
- It consisted of two stages: constant aerial bombardment and a ground offensive which lasted for just four days.
- Poorly managed and insufficiently prepared, the Iraqi troops were quickly swept away by the coalition.
- The outcome of the battle left Iraq battered, due to the destruction of its vital structures and an embargo on its

oil exports. Violent reprisals were held against internal rebellions in the north and south.

- Saddam Hussein was ultimately not ousted by the coalition, but was overthrown 13 years later, during the third Gulf War.
- A new order was established in the Middle East following the redistribution of oil export quotas and the growing influence of the United States.

FIND OUT MORE

BIBLIOGRAPHY

- Aburish, S.K. (2003) *Le vrai Saddam Hussein*. Paris: Saint-Simon.
- Chautard, S. (2003) *L'indispensable des conflits du XXe siècle*. Paris: Levallois-Perret.
- *Chroniques de la Guerre du Golfe* (1991) Paris: Édition Atlas.
- Ferrard, S. (1991) *Les armes de la guerre du Golfe*. Paris: Presses de la Cité.
- Gallois, P.-M. (2003) *Le sang du pétrole. Guerres d'Irak. 1990-2003*. Lausanne: L'âge d'homme.
- Guerre du Golfe (No date) *Chronologie de la Guerre du Golfe*. [Online]. [Accessed 7 December 2016]. Available from: <http://guerredugolfe.free.fr/>
- Jorgensen, C. (ed.) (2007) *Great Battles*. New York: Parragon Inc.
- July, S. (1991) *La diagonale du Golfe*. Paris: Grasset.
- Langendorf, J.-J. (1995) *Le bouclier et la tempête. Aspects militaires de la guerre du Golfe*. Geneva: Georg.
- Luizard, P.-J. (2002) *La question irakienne*. Paris: Fayard.
- Schwarzkopf, H.N. (1992) Mémoires. Paris: Plon.

ADDITIONAL SOURCES

- Mayika, K. and Al-Khalil, S. (1990) *Republic of Fear: The Inside Story of Saddam's Iraq*. New York: Pantheon Books.
- Schwarkzkopf, H.N. (1992) *It Doesn't Take a Hero*. New York: Bantam Books.

- Tucker-Jones, A. (2014) *The Gulf War: Operation Desert Storm 1990-1991*. Barnsley: Pen and Sword Military.

ICONOGRAPHIC SOURCES

- Logo of the United Nations (UN). Royalty-free reproduction picture.
- Emir Jaber al-Ahmad al-Sabah. © Pete Souza, official photographer of the White House.
- Saddam Hussein, 1979. © INA (Iraqi News Agency).
- General Herbert Norman Schwarzkopf (right) and General Colin Powell (left) during a press conference in February 1991. © PH2 SUSAN CARL.
- Pilot ready for takeoff during Operation Desert Storm, February 1991. © Staff Sgt. Lee F. Corkran.
- Military and civilian vehicles destroyed by the bombing attacks, 28 February 1991. © R.J. Worsley.
- Kuwaiti oil wells burned by Iraqi armed forces retreat, aerial view. © US Air Force.
- Kuwaiti oil wells burned by Iraqi armed forces retreat, terrestrial view. © JO1 Gawlowicz.
- Kurdish refugees fleeing Saddam Hussein's army thanks to allied support during Operation Provide Comfort, April 1991. © PHAN April Hatton.

FILMS AND DOCUMENTARIES

- *Courage Under Fire*. (1996) [Film]. Edward Zwick. Dir. USA: Davis Entertainment.
- *The Hidden Wars of Desert Storm*. (2001) [Documentary]. Audrey Brohy and Gérard Ungerman. Dir. USA.

- *Jarhead*. (2005) [Film]. Sam Mendes. Dir. USA: Red Wagon Entertainment, New Street Productions.
- *Dawn of the World*. (2007) [Film]. Abbas Fahdel. France/Germany/Iraq: ADR Productions, 27 Films Production.

MUSEUMS AND COMMEMORATIVE BUILDINGS

- Air Force Armament Museum, Florida (United States).
- Kuwait House of National Memorial Museum, Kuwait City (Kuwait).
- The Highway of Death, located between Kuwait and Iraq.
- Canadian War Museum, Ottawa (Canada).

IMPROVE YOUR GENERAL KNOWLEDGE

IN A BLINK OF AN EYE !

www.50minutes.com